Made in the USA
Las Vegas, NV
13 March 2022

45561782R00072